Nairn
Faces and Places

by David M. Ellen

European Library ZALTBOMMEL/THE NETHERLANDS

Acknowledgements:
For permission to use postcards and photographs and providing information the author wishes to thank: Nairn Fishertown Museum; Nairn Literary Institute Museum; Nairn Library; Firtree Publishing Ltd. Thanks are also due to the following people for their help: My wife Ara; my niece Jennifer Smith; Christina McDougall; John Lawson; Alan McGowan; Peter MacKenzie; Molly Cruickshank; Betty and John Cameron; Margaret Bochel; Alex Ross; David Mein; William Cope; Charles Robertson; Elma Webster; Ronald Watson; Janet Campbell; Bill Whyte, Peter Bradshaw, Hugh MacKenzie, John Semple, Ronald Gordon and Dan Morrison

Life's like a book where memory strays among remembered yesterdays.

GB ISBN 90 288 6022 3
© 1995 European Library – Zaltbommel/The Netherlands
Second edition, 1997: reprint of the original edition of 1995.

Introduction

Nairn is an ancient Burgh with records going back as far as the 13th century when it was called Invernairne. Its civic history begins with the creation of the Royal Burgh in the 12th century, when King David granted the original Royal Charter. The charter was later confirmed by King James in 1589, and the granting of the charter elevated Nairn to the status of a Royal Burgh, with many privileges that went with the royal recognition.

A charter granted by James I relates that 'the Burgesses of Nairn in all times past beyond the memory of all whomsoever were in use and possession of having and elected a Provost and Baillies, holding courts, administering justice, creating Burgesses, selling wine, wax, wool, cloth, fish, flesh and other merchandise and victuals, and holding and having workmen, of whatsoever kind, and also power of electing a representative to Parliament, of levying customs, anchorage and harbour dues on vessels using the harbour of the Burgh commonly reputed to the same'.

While preserving a monopoly of trade in the Burgh, the town did all in its power to enhance the importance of its markets, and these were held at Michaelmas. Three markets were held and they appear to have been attended by a large number of people. One of the duties of the Magistrates a day or two before the fair was to appoint a guard of twenty men to keep the peace of the market. The merchandise proper was confined to the booths on the High Street and the agricultural produce was sold at the Shambles Park, now the site of the Congregational Church.

The fair was really a business occasion and the bulk of the goods displayed were products of local industry. There was leather dressed and tanned, homespun cloth, plaidings, hose, wool, shawls and all types of wearing apparel. The small crofters in the upland of the county brought wooden tubs, cogs, and churns as well as farm produce. In 1750, the tolls of the market were let for £8 to £10 with each booth and stall-holder paying a few pence. There was also a weekly market held every Friday on High Street at which fleshers were obliged to present carcases for sale with hides uncut.

The weavers, who also appear to have engaged in the manufacture of linen, were a numerous class of tradesmen in the Burgh and the government encouraged the trade by introducing bounties. A favourite place for steeping the lint was where the water collected in pools of spring water along the links and Seabank lands. The name 'Lint Pots' was applied to the ground below Invernairn and Firthside. After the lint had been scutched, it was handed over to skilled hands to be heckled e.g., the finer spinning lint to be separated from the coarser tow. When finished, the lint was handed over to the women to be spun.

A peculiar duty carried out by Nairn Town Council in olden times, was that of supervising the quality of the ale brewed within the Burgh and, for that purpose, it had to be tasted. Ale brewing in those days was a staple industry and for the most part was carried on by women. Ale was usually made in three qualities, the weakest being termed ostler ale, the medium household ale being most widely used, and the strong ale which was only drunk on special occasions. In the 18th century, household ale was sold at twopence a pint and consequently became know as 'Twopenny', as mentioned in Burn's 'Tam O'Shanter'; 'Wi'ti-penny we fear nae evil.'

Notable among ancient municipal customs was the parade by the public drummer twice a day, once in the morning to arouse the inhabitants to their daily labour, and again at night to summon them to rest. In the

Council records of 21st October 1717, there occurs the following minute... 'The Council orders the Drummer to beat the taptoe and revalzie, as also the officer to ring the bell', the revalzie being the morning drum and the taptoe being the evening drum. In 1723, the town drum was either lost or stolen and an officer was appointed to get a warrant and search party and seek or seize the same wherever it may be found within the liberties of the Burgh. The result of the search is not recorded; it must, however, have been successful, as a town drum exists in the Nairn Museum.

A few miles from Nairn, numerous townships and villages existed, Auldearn and Cawdor being the largest of the townships. Maviston and Lochloy in the east were fishing villages. Merrietoun was located where once stood Merryton Farm and was thought to be the original fishertown when the river ran to the east. Milltoun was situated near to the town mill in Mill Road, where is now the playing field. Tamintoull was beside Meikle Balblair. Heathertoun was at the back of the ridge at Kildrummie. Cottertoun stood at the junction of the Ardersier and Inverness Road, and neighbouring it was Midtoun and Tamintoull between them. Further west on the Ardersier Road were Frasertoun and Croftoun, near the Kebbuck stone. A road led back from here along the base of the bluff towards Nairn, first passing Campbelltoun of Delnies, Fishertoun of Delnies and Hilltoun. On the south side of Nairn, there was Castletoun of Rait and Milltoun of Geddes, which was sometimes known as Kirktoun of Geddes.
The town of Nairn and its population has grown dramatically since those days. It would have been inconceivable to our forebears that Tradespark would be intergrated with the town and the farm of Achareidh a housing development.

Since earliest times the town had been concentrated on the west of the river, but now the policy of the District Council is to encourage development to the east. No doubt sometime in the future, and it is not too difficult to imagine, Auldearn will be part of the town of Nairn.

1   William Daniell's aquatint
of Nairn dated 1821 is taken
from his publication 'A Voyage Round Great Britain'. His
preliminary studies were
made during a series of journeys undertaken over a period
of twelve years, 1813-1825,
covering the entire coastline
of England, Wales and Scotland. His engravings provide a
fascinating record of the British coastal scene, its ports and
harbours, lighthouses, ships
and mariners in the early part
of the 19th century.

2 This view of Nairn High Street looking north was taken in the days when people had time to stand and stare, or perhaps it was the novelty of having their picture taken and they were told to stand perfectly still. The cottage with a tree in the garden stands on the site of the present Higgins building at the foot of Rose Street. The Station Hotel, later named the Highland Hotel, had not yet been built and Doctor Grigor had not arrived to stand at the junction of High Street and Leopold Street. Mrs. Orre's thatched cottage on the right, where now stands Burnett and Forbes, was removed in 1900. The Waverley Temperance Hotel sign is almost obscured by the branches of the large tree in Academy House garden. How nicely wooded the High Street was at that time.

3   This view of Nairn looking east in 1905 was taken from the roof of the parish church, from where a wonderful panoramic view of Nairn and environs can be had. There appears to be a great lack of trees in the outlying areas, although the town itself is well wooded. Ivybank House can be seen on the right with its extensive orchard, and Ivybank Cottages on Academy Street were removed for road improvements in the 1960's.

Nairn

Valentines Seri-s

4   Nairn High Street looking south about 1925. The first opening on the left of this view is the entrance to Castle Lane and the building on the far side of the lane, together with the row of houses, was demolished in the 1960's. On the immediate left was the Royal Bank of Scotland and next door was J. Michie, chemist. In Mackintosh's buildings on the right were Easiefit Shoes, Lipton the grocer and Alex Honeyman, draper.

5   An aerial view of Nairn looking west over the bridge before it was widened. The house in the foreground, '-Braehead', is in the course of construction which dates this view to 1931. Looking closely at this photograph today, many changes can be observed. Knowles and Cumming's lockups on the right no longer exist, Grant's garage in Harbour Street has been replaced by housing, and Mr. Cumming's house and cycle repair shop on the west side of the bridge has been replaced by Asher's bakery. The houses on the north side of Bridge Street were removed at the bridge widening.

6   John M. Cope, draper, with his staff, Lewis Robertson, Margaret Mein and Jack Mackintosh, in this photograph taken about 1929. John Cope favoured the trend customary at that time of displaying his wares hanging outside the premises. Tait and Ross, plumbers' shop on the opposite side of High Street, can be seen reflected in the window.

7   This is Urquharts the ironmongers and family grocers, where Woolworths is today on Nairn High Street. It may seem strange to the present generation and perhaps not very hygienic that this shop had ironmongery on one side and groceries on the other, but this was quite common practice in the period before the Second World War. A Secession Church once stood on the site of this shop which was the predecessor of the Rosebank Church.

8   Looking down King Street today, the only recognisable buildings in this view are the cottage at the end of Bath Street and the Congregational Church. The road widening carried out in 1962 saw the remaining buildings disappear. The wall on the right was the garden wall of Ashley, which is now a car park. The complete part of Macrae and Dick's Garage shown here was demolished, as also was Hugh Campbell's workshop, Colin Kinnaird's shop and the house at the foot of Douglas Street. The large house at the far end was the Congregational Church manse. A large part of the Glebe wall on the left was also demolished.

9   The reinforced concrete arches being constructed at the widening of the Nairn bridge which was started in 1936 and completed in 1937. A ceremony was held to mark the opening of the new bridge, and a director of the construction company presented Mrs. MacKay, the Provost's wife, with a silver quaich. The improvements to the bridge were a great success to the easier flow of traffic. The former proprietors of the shops that were demolished were relocated in High Street.

10   The staff of James Asher and Son, bakers, King Street, pose outside the bakery for this picture taken about 1919. Asher's bakery catered for most of the Fishertown weddings in the Seamen's Hall. In the Fishertown Museum there are several photographs of Asher's staff. Visitors to the museum are told that Ashers is the oldest bakery in the world, because they get a mention in the bible. It causes a lot of amusement when the visitors read in Genesis, chapter 49, verse 20: 'Out of Asher his bread shall be fat and he shall yield royal dainties.'

11   This is a view of Bridge Street about 1935, before the widening of the bridge over the river. This photograph was obviously taken on a Sunday, as the shops are closed and the children are dressed in their Sunday best. All the buildings along the left side of Bridge Street were removed and among the shops was a saddler, a fruiterer, a licensed grocer, a barber, a printer and a tailor. It was the custom when business closed on a Saturday to pull down the blinds in the shop windows, so as to shut off all signs of trade during the Sunday.

12   The two gentlemen on the right are very interested in the motor car passing down Nairn High Street, whereas the young girl is more interested in having her photograph taken. The archway at the far side of the Royal Hotel was the entrance to Macrae and Dick's Garage, which extended back to King Street and was formerly a stables and coach house. The tree on the left of this view was at the entrance of Ashley, the home of Asher the baker, which was formerly the manse of the Auld Kirk at the riverside.

13   Ivybank Lodge, which stood at the right-hand entrance to the present Rosebank School. Ivybank House was purchased by the Education Authority in 1927 in order to extend the Academy, and this lodge at the entrance gate was demolished at the same time as the house. Ivybank House was a military hospital during the First World War and many local ladies served there as auxiliary nurses.

14   This is the ruin of the old Secession Church, whose members were known as Seceders. The church was located in Castle Lane and stood there until it was demolished to make way for the telephone exchange in 1938. The church was formerly a stable with a thatched roof and earth floor. The first minister to be inducted there was the Rev. Isaac Ketchen in 1780, who remained for forty years. The congregation moved to a new church in Water Lane in 1820 and shortly afterwards Mr. Ketchen was succeeded by the Rev. James Mein, whose name some of the fisher families adopted.

15   This is Weaver's Vennel in Church Street before the cottages were removed to build the local council houses. It was here in this part of the town that the weavers carried out their trade. There were several vennels in Nairn at one time, but unfortunately the name fell into disuse. Jail Close was at one time called Free Kirk Vennel and is now Court House Lane. Douglas Street was once called Douglas Vennel and Church Street was for many years called Kirk Vennel.

16   Nothing now remains of Wordie's Cottages in Mill Road and the site where they stood is now plots. The tower in the skyline belonged to the Church Street School, which closed as a school about 1906. The building continued to be used for many years as a furniture store and workshop until it was destroyed by fire, and is now the present Tower Court. Wordies were the railway carters who delivered all heavy goods arriving by rail and they had their stables in Mill Road between the railway bridge and these houses. When the cottages were demolished, the tenants were rehoused in the council houses in Church Street.

17 This photograph entitled 'Children with driftwood at Nairn' was discovered together with 282 others in a photographic album in a second-hand bookshop in Stockport in 1986. The album was discovered by Bob Charnley, a retired policeman, who produced the best of the collection in a book entitled 'The Summer of '89' in which there are three photographs taken in Nairn. The album was called 'Scotch tour 1889' and the photographer was discovered to be Dr. Francis Smart from Tunbridge Wells, who made a summer tour of the Scottish Highlands with his family, travelling by train and stopping at interesting spots on the trip to pursue his hobby of photography.

18   The Cricket pitch on the links is regarded as being the most picturesque of all the north wickets, and cricket has been played here continuously for well over a hundred years. Cricket first came to Nairn when Englishmen working on the construction of the Inverness-Nairn railway line, applied to the Town Council for permission to remove the whin bushes, and flatten a piece of land to the east of the Bath Road, for the purpose of playing cricket. The present Cricket Pavilion is the third one to stand on the same site.

CRICKET ON LINKS, NAIRN

B 6044

19   Her Majesty Queen Elizabeth and Prince Philip paid an official visit to Nairn on 14th August 1961. The Royal visitors are seen here being greeted on the Links by the Lord Lieutenant of the County, Brig. Stirling, together with Provost Borthwick. The whole population of the town turned out to greet them and the school children had a holiday to celebrate the occasion. Some of the youth organisations in the town gave displays on the Links, the highlight of which was a breeches-buoy demonstration by the sea scouts.

20   There was a great exodus of young men from Nairn who emigrated to the colonies in the latter part of the 19th century, but many opted to stay in Scotland and seek fame and fortune in Glasgow. The Glasgow-Nairnshire Association was founded in 1870, when Mr. Samuel Fraser suggested to his fellow Nairnites working in Glasgow that they should widen their social circle, by looking out as many of the Nairn people as they could possibly find in Glasgow and have a soiree or supper to bring them together. Eighty men turned up at the Clarendon Café for their first meeting, and so was born the Glasgow-Nairnshire Association, which proved to be a great help in affording assistance in procuring situations for any who were unemployed, or found themselves in difficulties while resident in or passing through Glasgow.

DIRECTORS OF GLASGOW - NAIRNSHIRE ASSOCIATION
JUBILEE YEAR, 1920

21   This beautiful house, 'Glenridding', stood at the junction of King Street and Academy Street, facing along Leopold Street. This house was among several properties which were demolished in connection with the road improvements to King Street in 1962. The main purpose was to by-pass High Street and relieve it of the heavy through traffic.

22   Nairn Gas Works was established in 1842 and closed with the introduction of North Sea gas in the 1970's. Many poor families were kept warm during the winter with the coke gathered from the residue at the riverside wall. The gas works was a fascinating place for young boys and many found their way there on cold winter nights to watch the retorts being emptied and stoked with coal. One of the by-products was coal tar, which the fishermen used to tar their boats, fences and sheds.

23 The River Nairn looking south towards the Sewage Bridge and Road Bridge. It was unusual in later years for boats to be moored so far up river. The natural course of the river went eastwards just below the Sewage Bridge, meandering over the present flats of the Dunbar Golf Course and entering the sea below King's Steps at a point called the Watermouth. This estuary was where ships loaded and unloaded their cargoes until the latter part of the 18th century, when the estuary became silted up with sand and became too dangerous for shipping. It was then that the Town Council discussed the possibility of building a harbour, and when the harbour was eventually built in 1820, the river was then diverted to its present course.

NAIRN FROM THE MOUTH OF THE RIVER.

24   This is a view of Nairn Harbour in 1934, showing thirteen steam herring drifters and four line and lobster fishing boats. The smaller boats also fished the Kessock herring, which were plentiful in the shallow waters of the inner Firth until the 1960's. The steam drifter averaged eighty feet in length with an eighteen feet beam and a draught of eight to nine feet. Each drifter carried eighty to ninety nets, and each was about thirty-five yards long by fourteen yards deep and hung in the sea to trap the herring suspended by corks and buoys. A herring drifter carried a crew of nine including a skipper, a mate, an engineer, a stoker and a cook and four deck hands. These ships together with their crews saw naval service during both world wars.

25 This is the last of the oar propelled salmon fishing cobles operating from the shore. The dilapidated launching wheels look as if they have come to the end of their working life. Shortly after this time in 1962, the cobles were fitted with outboard motors and were moored in the harbour. At one time there were five salmon fishing stations operating between the Old Bar and Fort George, each employing five or six fishermen. Now the bothies are empty and the stations deserted due to the scarcity of salmon, caused in great measure, it is thought, by over-fishing and salmon netting in the North Sea.

26   The schooner 'Nairn-shire' was one of several owned by John Gordon and Son, coal and timber merchants. Coastal schooners of this type plied between the inner Moray Firth and north of England ports carrying mainly timber south and coal and lime north. Many ships of this type were built at Nairn, with the plentiful supply of wood from Cawdor and Darnaway Estates.

27 John Gordon and Sons' coal store at the corner of Harbour Street and Park Street, with the coal cart laden with bags of coal ready for delivery. Most of the coal in the early part of the century arrived by sailing schooners and was carted from the ships to this store for distribution. This site has now been developed for housing. Most of the lower end of Harbour Street near the harbour was lined with coal yards, builders' yards and fishermen's net and rope stores, until the area was cleared for housing development in 1990.

28 There were two salmon fishing stations on the Old Bar and this is the east bothy sheltered beneath the sand dunes. This was one of the most successful salmon stations which closed in the 1980's, along with many others in the inner Moray Firth. A mile further east was Shallowhead salmon station, where the wreck of an old sailing schooner appears from time to time. It was thought to be carrying coal from Brora to Findhorn and missed the opening to Findhorn bay in fog.

29   Most salmon fishing stations had their own ice-houses, particularly those in isolated bothies along the coast and where fresh water was available to make ice. They were usually built into a bank for coolness and covered on top with about a foot of turf. There was a small window or hatch at the rear, where the ice was admitted to the building. This ice was used to preserve the salmon before dispatch south during the warm summer months. The best preserved ice-houses are at Tugnet at the mouth of the river Spey, where huge catches of salmon were made and where there is now a Salmon Fishing Museum.

30   The Nairn herring drifter 'Narinia' entering the harbour at Great Yarmouth. This striking picture was featured in the Daily Mirror of 19th November 1937, under the caption 'Herrings are cheap today, lady. Remember the four plump herrings you bought for sixpence, Mrs. Housewife?' Now look at this picture of two herring drifters battling their way into port at Yarmouth. The crews have risked their lives for the catch in the raging gale, and now, at the very harbour mouth, great combers have nearly overwhelmed their little ships.

31   The English Church, which once stood at the corner of Bridge Street and Lochloy Road, is shown here in this photograph after it was shipped over to Lochinver and re-erected there. James Gordon, a native of Cawdor who in later years became a leading member of the Lochinver community, where they were in great need of a suitable place of worship, mentioned to his friends that the unused English Church in Nairn would suit them admirably. His brother John in Nairn arranged for the purchase and for the dismantling of the building, which was shipped round the Pentland Firth to Lochinver in the smack 'Snowdrop' and re-erected there. This view shows two Nairn fishing trawlers, Kilravock and Albion, moored at the pier at Lochinver with the Nairn church in the background, and two Nairn fishermen on the pier, Willie Duggie and Dod Storm.

32　Two Victorian ladies and a gentleman enjoying the benefit of the salubrious sea breezes about 1880. The life-boat house at the harbour is very prominent in this photograph and in the background is a schooner in the harbour. About this time, the Rt. Hon. Lord Thurlow extended the public promenade along the sea front past the Tortola well, at his own expense. It was thought that this improvement would add immensely to the pleasure and comfort of all who enjoy the walk at the seaside.

33   This is a group photograph of the Committee and Stewards at Nairn Farming Society's annual show. Seated are: Gus Morrison, Do Johnston, David MacArthur. George Innes, Secretary; Brig. Stirling, President; Andrew Wilson, Vice-President; James Philip and San Scott. The Society was founded on 8th November 1798, and its objects were the promotion of improvements in agriculture both by precept and example. Forty members joined at the first meeting and David Cruickshank, Lochloy, was appointed President. The first show of young cattle was held at Clephanton in 1819, and subsequent shows were held at various parts of the County until the present field was purchased and established as the regular venue.

34   Viewfield Lodge stood at the entrance to Viewfield House, on the site of the present Police Buildings and was demolished during the 1962 road improvements, when the whole of King Street was widened. Although the wall and gate pillars were rebuilt, the lovely stone urns on the pillars unfortunately disappeared.

35   Merryton Stores, which stood at the junction of the Forres Road and Lochloy Road, was built by Provost William Mackenzie in 1931 to serve Broadhill and the recently-built Merryton Crescent. The stone for the building was the last to be quarried at Lochloy. The building, which was built by Alexander MacGillivray, was demolished in 1983 because of the ever increasing traffic and the need for road improvements.

36   This view of Dulsie Bridge on the river Findhorn is unusual, because it includes Dulsie Farm house. The bridge is often referred to as a General Wade bridge, when in fact it was built by his successor Major William Caulfield. The military road from Perth to Fort George was constructed between 1748 and 1757. Dulsie Bridge was built to span the river Findhorn high above its scenic rocky gorges and carries Caulfield's road over and up past the house which you see here, which was the King's House or Inn in the 18th century. Robert Burns stayed here during his Highland tour in 1787.

DULSIE BRIDGE, RIVER FINDHORN.

With best wishes for all good things at Christmas + a bright + happy 1908 -   M. Douglas.

37   Nairn Railway Viaduct was designed by Joseph Mitchell and built in 1857 for the Inverness and Aberdeen Junction Railway. He described the work on this bridge as heavy and formidable. The side flood arch was constructed to take the mill lade from the town meal mill and later from the Glen Cawdor Distillery, which stood on the site of the present playing field. The stone used in the building of the viaduct was from the Lochloy Quarry and Mr. Squair, Nairn, was the building contractor.

38   This group of sea scouts are seen here with their Scoutmaster, Alex Heard, and two Assistant Scoutmasters, Jack Bunker and Bill Shaw. This troop, together with a troop of first Nairnshire Boy Scouts, travelled by bus to the Empire Exhibition at Bellahouston Park, Glasgow, in 1938. It was a great experience for the boys because, apart from Scout camps, it was the farthest they had ever travelled from home. The troop stayed for a week in a Scout Hall in Old Hall Road in Paisley and visited the exhibition every day.

39 The 1st Nairnshire Boy Scout Troop lead the procession in the parade to celebrate the coronation of King George V on 23rd June 1911. Mr. Riach, headmaster of the Church Street School, was Scout Master, and he can be seen at the rear of the troop. The 1st Nairnshire Troop is said to be the oldest in existence in the British Isles.

40   Nairn Parish School was founded in 1762 and was a fee paying school which produced many fine scholars. An article published about 1800 said: 'In the town of Nairn is an excellent school in which the number of scholars is seldom under one hundred. Parents send children thither from all parts of the country and frequently even from England. Every branch of study now in repute at universities is taught here to perfection. Several of the most distinguished characters for science and literature in Great Britain first rose to comparative eminence in the provincial school of Nairn.' By the time this photograph was taken, the school was closed and the building used as an auction room. The shop of George Whyte, cabinetmaker and upholsterer, now stands on the site of the old school.

41   The Nairn Fishermen's Flute Band flourished in the 1890's under its conductor Hector Ross, seated on left. Nairn Seaman's Hall Total Abstinence Society was formed in 1879 and it was a tradition to carry the temperance flag 'We Will Stick To Our Pledge' throughout the town every New Year's Day, preceded by the Fishermen's Flute Band and sometimes a piper. Those who marched behind the banner pledged total abstinence, identified by a blue ribbon in their buttonhole. This practice continued until 1912.

42   The newly-formed
Nairn Pipe Band with their
new uniforms, pipes and
drums posing on the putting
green for their first official
photograph. The band was
formed in 1934 and at first
paraded and marched up and
down High Street on a Saturday evening without uni-
forms. By the following year
sufficient funds had been
raised to purchase uniforms
and equipment and the band
was officially established and
held their inaugural parade
on 21st July 1935.

43 The Nairn Pipe Band under the command of Drum-Major William Urquhart and Pipe-Major William MacKenzie, consisted of fourteen pipers and ten drummers, and with the band's highland dancers, chaperoned by Mrs. Daly, went on tour to South Wales on 4th June 1965. This ambitious enterprise was made possible through the sponsorship of Mr. Peter MacGillivary, a Nairnite who emigrated to Swansea in 1919, and had never forgotten his affection for his native town. The band and dancers performed at five different venues and were warmly received everywhere they went. At the front of the photograph can be seen Mr. Peter MacGillivary, Provost Knowles of Nairn, the Mayor of Swansea, and Mrs. MacGillivary.

44 The Royal Marine Hotel, and in the foreground the flooded quarry hole before it was drained into the sea and the putting green, then constructed on top of the filled-in quarry hole. John Cope, a local business man and member of the Burgh Council, conceived the idea of making a putting green and at the same time solving a problem which had been troubling the council of eliminating a dangerous play area for children. The stone for the building of the Marine Hotel and some of the nearby houses came from this quarry.

45   A view of the interior of Nairn Salt Water Swimming Baths which was the second swimming baths to be built on this site. It advertised hot and cold douche and sea-weed, pine and sulpher baths. A fine swimming club and water polo team associated with the baths were promi-nent with displays during the swimming galas held every summer, during the years between the two world wars. School children of all ages were taught to swim and if frightened of the water, they were placed in a harness sus-pended from a long pole and paddled until they gained confidence. The swimming baths were requisitioned by the military during the Second World War, and after the war extensive renovations were carried out to restore them to their former condition.

46   Nairn Railway Station staff in 1938 were: David Taylor, Jean MacGillivray (Menzies Book Shop), David Grant, Dan MacMillan, Sandy (Napper) Thompson, John Campbell (station master), Charlie Morrison and Hugh MacDonald. In July 1969, part of the film 'The Private Life of Sherlock Holmes' was filmed at Nairn station. At that time, Inverness station had recently been modernised and Nairn station, which still retained its Victorian façade, was chosen to represent Inverness station. Passengers on the Aberdeen-Inverness train were amazed to find themselves in a strange Inverness station. The principals in the film were Christopher Lee, Robert Stephens, Colin Blakely and Genevieve Page, and Nairn Drama Club members were extras in the film. The film is frequently shown on television.

47 Members of the Nairn wartime National Fire Service Fire Brigade pose for this photograph at the fire station at the old Monitory School, Harbour Street, in November 1944. The names from left back are: John MacGillivray, Bimbo Morganti, Christie Macrae, Alex Nicolson, Harry Neville, Willie Grey, Alex MacIntyre, Jock MacRonald, Ackie Macrae, Alex Murray, Margaret Ross, Davie Campbell, Angus Innis, Dan MacDonald (Fire Master), James Ross, John Finlayson and Mary Menzies.

48   Queen Victoria was celebrating her 80th birthday on 24th May 1899, when the first ball was struck to celebrate the opening of the Nairn Dunbar Golf Course. The year 1907 proved to be significant for the club when at a cost of £193 6s. 1d., a new clubhouse was built. Over the years the clubhouse had been considerably extended, and in this photograph taken in the 1950's, we see the original clubhouse with a small lounge extension built in the 1930's.

49 A view of Nairn Golf Clubhouse looking east in 1906, with the old professional shop and caddy shed in the background. Young boys from the age of ten were in great demand as caddies during the summer school holidays in July and August. The basic rate for a junior caddy was 1/3d., but most golfers paid 2/- or 2/6d., and sufficient money could be saved to pay for school books and a complete new outfit of clothes, especially a blue burberry for the new school term. Seabank Road was being developed about this time and a striking feature of this view is the great lack of trees and shrubbery.

Nairn.

Golf Course

50   Many Nairn servicemen who served in the Middle East during the Second World War were surprised to find Nairn Transport Co. buses running between Damascus and Bagdad, a distance of 630 miles over the desert. The company was started by Norman Nairn, a New Zealander, who after service in the First World War remained in the Middle East. He was convinced that it was possible to traverse the desert by wheeled traffic rather than the slow mode of traffic by camel. Backed by the Iraqi Government, he gained a five year contract for the carriage of mails between Bagdad and Haifa. When the desert warfare broke out in the Middle East during the Second World War, the Nairn Transport Company proved to be invaluable to the Allied cause with their superior knowledge of the Sahara Desert.

The biggest bus in the world in its time: a thirty-six seater carrying a buffet and

51   A large and colourful parade was held in Nairn on 3rd June 1953 to celebrate the coronation of Queen Elizabeth II. Sir Gordon Richards, who had been knighted in the Coronation Honours List, won the Derby on 'Pinza' on his 28th attempt. Here Alex Bochel and David Ellen are tipping Pinza to win. Pinza, the 5 to 1 favourite, dictated the race by taking the lead a quarter of a mile from home and won by four lengths!

52 The River Nairn in spate in 1956 caused a considerable amount of damage all along the banks and particularly at Househill, where it breached the east bank and flooded a large area from below the cemetery to the Crook. It took two years work to restore the damage done and secure the banks to withstand any future extreme conditions.

53   A close-up of the river in spate at the Sewage Bridge. It was feared that this bridge would be carried away under the onslaught of the raging water. It, however, withstood the pounding, reinforced by the large sewage pipe carried on its undercarriage. The Shambles in the centre of the picture has now been demolished, giving a clear view of Merryton Farm House. Merryton Farm buildings on the left were demolished in the seventies and a private housing development built on the site.

54 On 15th May 1934, the Nairn High Church Choir competed in the Inverness Music Festival with great success, ably conducted by Mr. Alfred Dinsdale, organist and choir master of the church. They competed against choirs from Beauly and Dingwall in the class for church choirs. The Nairn choir secured the premier place by winning the Leys Castle Trophy for the second year. The two sacred pieces which the choir rendered were 'O' Lord Support Us' and 'God So Loved the World', and both were sung unaccompanied.

55   The Nairn Male Voice Choir under its conductor William Cameron seen here with the Highland Light Infantry Band from Fort George at a concert in the Public Hall, in 1934. This choir was renowned throughout the North of Scotland for the quality of its singing and was in great demand for charity concerts. The Military Bands from Fort George always welcomed the opportunity to display their professional musical abilities to the general public and their presence was always welcome, and their music much appreciated.

56   Nairn Motor Garage was owned by Knowles and Cumming who were also proprietors of the sports and cycle shop on Bridge Street. This picture, taken about 1920, would appear to be in the month of August, when the holiday parties were up north for the shooting season bringing with them their motor cars and chauffeurs.

57 Ardclach Bell Tower, reputed to be the highest belfry in Scotland, was originally used as a state prison by the Laird of Leven who was the patron of Ardclach Church and a staunch Covenanter. He allowed the Church Session to use the building from time to time, first as a place of confinement for the moral delinquents, and afterwards as a bell-house because of its proximity to the church. The elevated situation enabled the bell tower to be used as a lookout post for cattle reivers, who made regular forays along the Findhorn valley. In the Presbytery records, there is reference to two bells, a large and a small one, but they were torn down long ago and thrown into the river by a band of Lochaber reivers who took exception to the alarm signals they gave out.

58　This view of Nairn harbour about 1890 shows part of the fishing fleet consisting mainly of Zulu herring sailing drifters. The Zulu boat superseded the Scaffie in popularity and was thought to be a vastly superior sailing drifter. The first Zulu was designed by William Campbell of Lossiemouth at the time of the Zulu wars in 1879, hence the name.

59   The west pier of Nairn Harbour seen here in this view taken about 1880, was designed by Thomas Telford, the famous engineer who built the Caledonian Canal. The pier acted as a refuge from the strong prevailing westerly winds where the boats could moor and shelter in safety. Unfortunately, the great Moray Flood of 1829 caused extensive damage to the pier which lay in a derelict condition for several years until sufficient funds were raised to restore it and at the same time build another breakwater at the east side. About this time, many families came into Nairn from the outlying fishing villages, where bigger boats could be moored and a ready market was available for their catches.

60   A group of workmen at the building of the new harbour, completed and officially opened in August 1932, by Lady Grant of Logie. The steam pile driver seen in the picture was operated only at ebb tide, day and night, much to the annoyance of the folk who lived near the harbour, whose sleep was continually disturbed. The building of the new harbour caused a great deal of public feeling and controversy, and the general feeling was that it was built too late to be of much benefit to the fishing industry, which was by then on the decline.

61   Up until the First World War, the fishertown of Nairn was a little world of its own, a tight-knit community caught up in the relentless seagoing way of life. The neighbourly style in which the houses were built reflects this as in this view of a close in Park Street, built side by side with smoking sheds for curing the fish and sheds for storing lines and nets. The fishertown was a self-contained community with five shops and ship chandlers, who literally stocked everything, from a needle to an anchor. The ships' supplies and gear were usually given on credit until they returned from a fishing trip.

62 Jeemes and Willie Wallace were the last of the Nairn line fishermen. Willie was deaf and dumb and Jeemes had an impediment in his speech. They owned a small Zulu boat called the 'Water Lily' and were loved by generations of children, who were thrilled to be invited out for a sail in their boat. Many rescues were carried out by the Wallace brothers of young, foolhardy boys, who would drift out to sea in rowing boats and in home-made rafts. The brothers and their boat were in great demand during the visit of the Home Fleet to the Moray Firth, when they ran trips out to the battleships anchored in the Firth.

63 Mr. and Mrs. Mackintosh, Park Street, are seen here redding and baiting their small lines which were used for catching haddock, whiting and small flat fish. Each fisherman had a line of fifty fathoms (300 ft) in length and attached to each of these lines were one hundred snoods. Snoods were lines from two to three feet long carrying the baited hooks. Each line was laid clear in a scue, i.e. a flat basket, so that they could be run out clearly as the boat sailed along.

64   Six Nairn fisher lassies with three coopers at Fraserburgh. They are: Mattie Bochel, Nana Baillie, Mima Ellen, Bessie Bochel, Maggie Laird and Maggie Main. Hundreds of Scottish fisher girls were employed in gutting, packing and salting the herring in barrels to be exported abroad, mainly to Russia and Germany. They worked in teams of three, two gutters and a packer, and sometimes worked from dawn to dusk until all the herring had been cured. The work was hard and poorly paid, but the girls enjoyed the freedom of being away from home in Fraserburgh, Shetland, Yarmouth, Ireland and the Isle of Man.

65   The 'Dunlogie' was the last boat to be built at Walker's boat building yard at Nairn harbour. It was also the first seine net fishing boat to be built for Nairn fishermen in 1934. Nairn subsequently had a large fleet of seine net trawlers which were mostly built at Herd and Mackenzie's yard at Buckie. The boats built at the north-east coast yards were regarded as being second to none for quality.

66   Elsie Callie, a typical Nairn fishwife, who together with her sister purchased, cured and smoked her Nairn speldings and sold them to her regular customers throughout the town and county. The fishwives would regularly barter their fish for country produce such as eggs, butter, oatmeal and potatoes, and would arrive back home laden with as much weight as they left with in the morning. The coming of the railway in the middle of the 19th century was a great boon to the fishwives with the ready available market in Inverness and Speyside. Two days after the Inverness-Nairn railway line was opened on 15th November 1855, twenty-two Nairn fishwives travelled to Inverness each carrying about one cwt. of fish.

67   Two Nairn fishwives, Annie Ralph and Nan Bunker, selling their speldings (haddocks, split, salted and smoked in durkins or fir cones) from the seats in front of the Court House in the 1930's. In the year 1711, the relations between the fishers and the upper part of the town were considerably strained as explained in a Town Council minute of that year. 'Complaints being made that the fishers carried their fish to the country and obliged the inhabitants to go down to the shore to buy their fish at their houses, to the great prejudice of the town in hindering the country people to frequent it, do therefore appoint that all fishers henceforth be obliged to sell none of their fish till they come to the cross before going to the country.'

68   Nairn fishermen and boys posing for a photograph at the harbour in front of two Zulu fishing boats about 1902. The turn of the century began to see the demise of the sail fishing boats with the advent about this time of the steam drifter. And so began the most prosperous time in the herring fishing from 1900 until the outbreak of the First World War in 1914, when the Russian and German markets for salt herring were lost. All the steam drifters were confiscated for war service, some to Invergordon, some to Scapa Floe as supply ships, and some to the Mediterranean as mine sweepers. The herring fishing industry never really recovered its former prosperity and slowly went into decline until the introduction of the seine net trawlers in the late 1920's and 1930's.

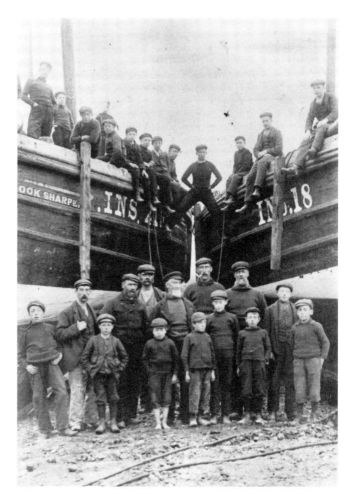

69   This is a view of Falconer's Lane looking east before the cottages on the left were removed to make the car-park. Very little now remains of the lane as it was in former times. A blacksmith's existed here for centuries and in former times was a farrier's and sword sharpener's. The lane had for many years a baker's shop and a public house at each end, one of which was called the Vine. There may have been some connection between Falconer's Lane and Falconer's Park, which was located to the east of the Star Hotel in Church Street, where public gatherings were held, and was the venue for travelling circuses before the Links was cleared of whins.

70   This unusual view taken from a window of Lothian House shows the entrance to Kingillie House. The Marine Road housing development on Kingillie orchard had not yet been started when this picture was taken. Kingillie House, a part of which can be seen, is an eighteenth century house and one of the oldest properties in Nairn. The castellated rear wing is probably a later addition, but is shown in Wood's map of 1821. The Marine Hotel spire in the background was later destroyed by fire.

71   This view of Nairn beach on a busy, sunny August day in 1930 is how the older generation remember the school summer holidays. In Victorian and Edwardian times the bathing machines were pulled into the sea and out again by horses, after the bathers had their dip. When this picture was taken, the bathing coaches as they were then called, were fixtures on the beach and families spending the day at the seaside used them as a base and changing rooms. Daily, weekly or season tickets could be purchased for the coaches. They disappeared with the outbreak of the Second World War.

THE CALL OF THE SEASIDE, NAIRN

72   The great Culbin disaster, which completely inundated the entire estate of Culbin in a sand storm, happened in 1694. The estate consisted of sixteen farms, a mansion house and orchard, crofts and farm workers' cottages. The sand encroached on the arable land for the first time in 1676 and every succeeding year the problem increased. The great storm of 1694 was sudden and unexpected, blowing from the west and taking everyone by surprise. The wind continued to blow the sand eastwards for a period of several days, blocking the estuary of the river Findhorn and changing the course of the river to the east away from the Old Bar. When the storm eventually blew itself out, 3,000 acres of arable land were lost for ever. The Forestry Commission purchased the eight square miles of sand-dunes in 1930 and stabilised the sand by planting trees with great success.

Culbin Sands, near Forres. "Buried Beneath This Desert Are Farms, Villages And One Time Fertile Fields." 19.

73   When Nairn's first tar boiler came to the town in the 1920's, it was a great source of attraction for the children. It was thought that the vapour from the boiling tar was good for curing whooping cough and children were brought along to benefit from inhaling the tar fumes if the boiler was in the vicinity. The Gas Works, too, was a favourite place to take children to be cured by the fumes from the gas retorts and from the steam from the cooling coke. In this photograph, Mr. Peter, Burgh Surveyor, on the right, is inspecting the work.

74   Geordie Patience was one of Nairn's worthies who was never known to have done a day's work in the whole of his life. He lived entirely on his wits, and had a glib tongue and personality which made him acceptable and tolerated by everyone. He lived for many years in a hut at the Lochloy quarries with a sign over the door 'Sleepy Valley', named after a popular song of the time. Geordie had a good singing voice and was often invited to perform in Scout gangshows, singing his favourite song 'Goodbye, Old Ship O'Mine'.

75   William Gordon, affectionately known throughout the town as 'Tiptoe'. He was born in Balblair Home, where a young girl who was nursing him fractured his foot trying to squeeze it into a button boot. Before it was realised what was wrong with the child, it was too late and he was a cripple for the rest of his life. Willie lived on his wits, doing a bit of fishing and rabbit trapping and chatting up any visitors at the harbour who would listen to his weird and imaginary tales. He lived for many years in an old Lipton's van in a yard at the harbour before moving to Lochloy quarry and finally to a caravan site on the busy Inverness Road, where he was killed in a road accident.

76 These four itinerant tinkers were well-known throughout the Highlands, never staying very long in one place. Many tinkers were excellent tinsmiths, who repaired kitchen utensils and sharpened knives and scissors. Woollen rags could be exchanged for balloons and goldfish, which were very popular with the children. Many tinkers were fine horse breeders and were at one time the main dealers in ponies. There were two lodging houses in Nairn in the years between the wars where itinerant tramps could find lodgings. These gentlemen of the road were sometimes referred to as 'Milestone Inspectors'.